SURVIVOR

John F. Kennedy and PT109

Philip Abraham

HIGH
interest
books

Children's Press®
A Division of Scholastic Inc.
New York / Toronto / London / Auckland / Sydney
Mexico City / New Delhi / Hong Kong
Danbury, Connecticut

Book Design: Laura Stein, Christopher Logan, and Erica Clendening
Contributing Editor: Matthew Pitt

Photo Credits: Cover, pp. 4, 11, 20, 31, 34 © Corbis; Back cover, pp. 1, 5, 9, 17, 27, 35, 40–48 © Digital Vision; p. 7 © Hulton/Archive by Getty Images; pp. 8, 14, 16, 25 courtesy of the U.S. Naval Historical Center; pp. 13, 26, maps by Erica Clendening; p. 23 © Everett Collection; p. 33 © Elliot Erwitt/Magnum Photos; p. 37 © Robert Knudsen, White House/John F. Kennedy Library, Boston; p. 38 © AP/Wide World Photos

Library of Congress Cataloging-in-Publication Data

Abraham, Philip, 1970–
John F. Kennedy and PT109 / by Philip Abraham.
    p. cm. — (Survivor)
Includes bibliographical references and index.
Summary: Relates the courage of John F. Kennedy during World War II, especially in saving his crew when they were stranded in the South Pacific after their PT boat was rammed by a Japanese warship.
    ISBN 0-516-23905-8 (lib. bdg.) — ISBN 0-516-23487-0 (pbk.)
    1. Kennedy, John F. (John Fitzgerald), 1917–1963—Career in the Navy. 2. Kennedy, John F. (John Fitzgerald), 1917–1963—Military leadership. 3. World War, 1939–1945—Naval operations, American. 4. World War, 1939–1945—Pacific Ocean. [1. Kennedy, John F. (John Fitzgerald), 1917–1963. 2. World War, 1939–1945—Naval operations, American. 3. World War, 1939–1945—Pacific Ocean.] I. Title. II. Series.

E842.3 .A28 2002
940.54'5973—dc21

                                                    2001042351

Contents

Introduction

The impact of a sudden collision throws you against the rear of your boat's cockpit. Your back slams against steel. The pain is beyond words. You cannot believe what is happening—a Japanese warship has rammed your PT boat. Flames surround you. You realize that your boat might explode. Fighting back your pain, you order your crew to abandon ship.

You jump overboard with the crew and soon break the water's surface—eyes stinging, throat burning, back aching. Dancing flames light the blackened night sky. The Japanese warship is long gone. You shout for your crew. Only a few of them answer. Some are badly hurt. If you don't do something, you will all die at sea. But how does one person save twelve others? *How will you survive the night?*

 PT boats like the one in this painting were used by the United States to win World War II.

These are just some of the things that the young captain of PT109 had to deal with on the night his boat was sunk. Before he was president of the United States, John F. Kennedy was a lieutenant in the U.S. Navy during World War II. Kennedy's actions during this crisis changed him from a PT-boat skipper into a war hero.

This book will explore one of the most dramatic events of World War II—how John F. Kennedy saved his crew.

John F. Kennedy served in the U.S. Navy before beginning his political career. ▶

One

Background to Danger

World War II was fought from 1939 to 1945. It pitted the countries of Germany, Italy, and Japan against nations such as Great Britain, the United States, and the Soviet Union. Up until 1941, the United States refused to join the war. Then, on December 7, 1941, Japanese planes bombed the U.S. naval base at Pearl Harbor, Hawaii. This sneak attack killed 2,400 servicemen. It also destroyed much of the U.S. fleet of ships in the South Pacific Ocean. The bombing of Pearl Harbor brought the United States into the fight.

Japan attacked the United States from different areas in the South Pacific. The U.S. Navy sent many ships to this area to stop further attacks. The mission was simple—stop the Japanese at all costs.

The U.S.S. Shaw explodes during the Japanese attack on Pearl Harbor, December 7, 1941.

By 1943, the navy had set up bases throughout the South Pacific. The navy used many types of ships to fight the Japanese forces, including destroyers, aircraft carriers, and PT boats.

PT BOATS

PT boats were small ships that could move faster than larger ships. "PT" stands for Patrol Torpedo. The hull, or body, of a PT boat was made from wood. Boats made from wood are lighter than steel boats.

PT boats used torpedoes as their main weapons. A torpedo is like an underwater rocket. The tip of a torpedo is called the warhead. The explosives are kept in this part. The back end of a torpedo has a propeller with a motor. The motor causes the propeller blades to spin. The spinning blades move the torpedo through the water toward its target. PT boats patrolled waterways where enemy ships were known to travel. When an enemy ship was spotted, a PT boat would fire torpedoes at it.

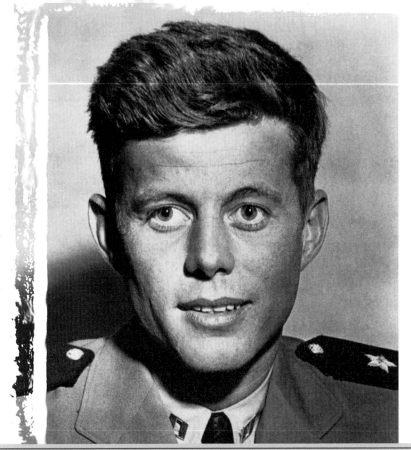

At a young age, Kennedy responded to the call to defend his country.

JFK

John Fitzgerald Kennedy was the second of nine children born to Joseph and Rose Kennedy. The Kennedys were a wealthy family. They lived in Boston, Massachusetts. John was a bright young man who was eager to serve his nation.

After the attack on Pearl Harbor, John tried to join the army. He decided this would be the best way to serve his country. However, the army would not take him because he had a bad back. He'd hurt his back playing football while attending Harvard University. But John was determined to be a part of the war effort. For five months, he did special exercises to strengthen his back. The exercises worked. This time, he applied to the navy. He was accepted. Because John had a lifelong love of the sea, the navy was a perfect fit.

John taught at the navy's torpedo boat training school. He was a good teacher, but he

Did you know?

The U.S. Navy often uses code words while in battle. In navy slang, torpedoes are called "fish."

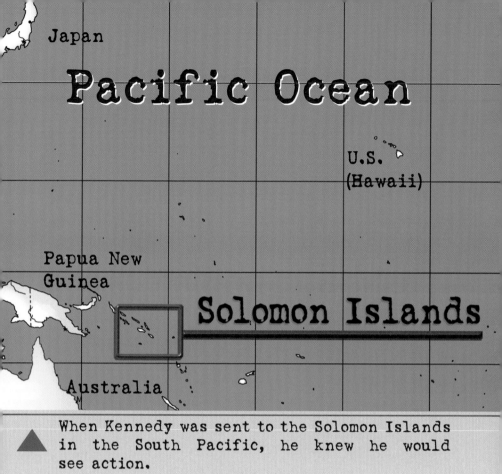

Japan

Pacific Ocean

U.S.
(Hawaii)

Papua New
Guinea

Solomon Islands

Australia

▲ When Kennedy was sent to the Solomon Islands in the South Pacific, he knew he would see action.

wanted to see action in the war. He asked his father to use his influence with top naval officials. Joseph Kennedy knew many people in government. He had been the United States ambassador to England from 1937 to 1940. Joseph got his son a transfer to the Solomon Islands in the South Pacific.

TOUGH CONDITIONS

Rendova is one of the Solomon Islands. The main base for torpedo boats was located there. Living on Rendova during the war was no paradise. The weather was always hot and sticky. Bugs and rats were everywhere. Some men's skin turned yellowish from the medicine they took to prevent malaria. Malaria is a disease spread by mosquito bites that can cause horrible chills and fever in humans. The food was awful, boring, or both. The meals were usually made from the tinned meat called SPAM.

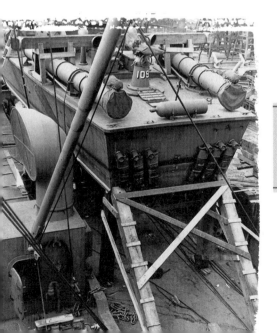

 Kennedy and his crew worked hard to get their craft battle-ready.

The living quarters were also bad. Most crews lived on their PT boats. The boats were cramped and smelly.

John Kennedy saw the poor living conditions as a challenge. He was determined to make things better for his new crew. He quickly impressed them with his intelligence and sense of humor. He made them feel good about themselves. Together, they got PT109 into fighting shape.

Did you know?

Kennedy loved sweets. While in the South Pacific, he developed a taste for powdered ice cream. The powder was mixed with water and poured into an ice-cube tray. The mixture was frozen in PT109's small refrigerator. Kennedy would eat bowls of it as he piloted PT109.

Two

Doomed Patrol

Afternoon, August 1, 1943
The base commander, Thomas G. Warfield, received a message. It reported that there was a good chance that Japanese destroyers would be in the area. These warships were carrying troops and supplies. The message also stated that Japanese planes, called dive-bombers, were in the air looking for PT boats to attack.

Soon after Warfield got the message, Japanese dive-bombers attacked the PT base. PT109 had been in the harbor waiting to have maintenance work done. When the attack started, Kennedy moved PT109 out of the harbor. At the same time, his crew opened fire on the planes. They trained guns from PT109's deck on the enemy fighter planes. They did their best to fight off the

On August 1, base commander Thomas Warfield barely had time to warn PT109's crew of a surprise Japanese attack.

THE PT109 CREW

- John F. Kennedy, Captain
- George Henry Robertson Ross
- John E. Maguire
- Harold W. Marney
- Leonard J. Thom
- Edgar E. Mauer
- Charles A. Harris
- Patrick McMahon
- William Johnston
- Gerald E. Zinser
- Raymond Starkey
- Andrew Jackson Kirksey
- Raymond Albert

You can learn more about this heroic crew from the Web sites in the back of this book.

dive-bombers. The attack was quickly over, but it took a toll on the PT boats and their crews. PT164 was blown up. Two of its crew were killed. Kennedy's PT109 crew had escaped the danger.

Night, August 1

That night, every PT boat was ordered on patrol. There were fifteen boats in all. The boats were divided up into four groups. Each group had an area in the Blackett Strait to patrol. Their job was to do as much damage as possible to nearby Japanese ships.

Early Morning, August 2

Shortly after midnight, PT159 spotted Japanese warships. At first the crew thought that the warships were only barges. They soon realized they were wrong. In the confusion of the battle that followed, PT159 did not alert the other PT boats.

However, PT157's crew saw what was happening and raced to join the battle. Off in the distance, Kennedy and his crew could see flashes of light. At first they thought it was coming from Japanese bases. When some of the shell bursts came near PT109, Kennedy called for "general quarters." This meant the crew had to prepare for battle immediately. PT109's radioman received a message from a

As they patrolled the South Pacific on August 2, the PT109 crew had no clue they would soon be attacked by the *Amagri*.

PT boat captain: "I am being chased through Ferguson Passage. Have fired fish."

PT109 met up with PT162 and PT169. There was much confusion. No one knew what was going on. They knew there was fighting nearby, but they didn't know exactly where. No official word came from the PT base. Finally, the three captains radioed the base for further orders. They were told to resume their normal patrol stations.

PT109 went back on patrol. The crew was still unaware that Japanese destroyers were lurking in the area. This moment of calm was about to be shattered.

Out of nowhere, a large dark shape sprang up on PT109's starboard bow. *Starboard* refers to the boat's right side, and *bow* refers to the boat's front. The destroyer sliced through the ocean quickly. It was 300 yards (274 m) away and closing in fast. The alarm sounded. The crew went into action.

PT109 started to turn starboard, or right, so that the torpedoes could be fired. The boat couldn't turn fast enough, though. In mid-turn, PT109 was rammed by the Japanese destroyer, *Amagri*. The *Amagri* collided with PT109 diagonally. The force of the impact ripped the PT boat into two parts. As the huge destroyer lumbered past PT109, it fired twice. Luckily, both shots missed.

The ramming of PT109 created a fire. Gasoline from the ruptured gas tanks burned on the water's surface. The crew was saved from the fire because the wake of the destroyer pulled most of the burning gas away from PT109.

During the collision, Kennedy was thrown against the back of the cockpit. The impact hurt his back. Though the boat was cut in half, the bow didn't sink. Only Kennedy, Thom, Ross, Mauer, McGuire, and Albert managed to hold onto the bow. The others were thrown into the fiery waters.

Soon the men abandoned the bow because it looked as if the fire in the water would spread to it. Once that danger passed, they climbed back on. Kennedy and the others shouted for the missing crewmen. Kennedy swam 100 yards (91 m) southwest to Harris, McMahon, and Starkey. Thom and Ross swam southeast to get Zinser and Johnston.

Kennedy sized up the situation. He saw that McMahon was badly burned and in the worst shape of all his men. Starkey had also been burned. Kennedy had Harris and Starkey stay where they were while he took McMahon back to PT109. It was not an easy swim. Kennedy had to be careful not to cause McMahon more pain.

The awesome impact of the *Amagri* colliding with PT109 tore the small boat in half in just 10 seconds.

Kennedy also had to swim against the current. It took him an hour to get back to PT109. Kennedy left McMahon with the others on board. He went back for Harris and Starkey.

Fighting his pain, fear, and exhaustion, Kennedy continued his dangerous swim across the dark waters. It took three tiring hours for him to gather the survivors. Marney and Kirksey were never found. It is believed they were killed during the collision.

The eleven survivors were not out of danger. They were injured and had no first-aid kit. There was no food or fresh water, either. The waters were rough and shark-infested. Two Japanese

bases were mere miles away, on the islands of Gizo and Kolombangara. Worst of all, there was no sign that the navy had sent out a search party to rescue the PT109 crew.

Late Morning, August 2

Kennedy and his crew stayed on PT109 through the morning. They knew they couldn't stay on the ship much longer. It had started to take on water and would eventually sink. They were hoping to be spotted by a naval plane, but none flew overhead. Swimming to a nearby island seemed to be their best hope for survival.

Afternoon, August 2

Kennedy decided to lead his crew to one of the smaller islands southeast of Gizo. He chose Plum Pudding Island. He believed it was less likely to be occupied by Japanese forces.

They set out in the early afternoon. Kennedy led the way. To save the badly burned McMahon,

A life jacket like this one, combined with Captain Kennedy's strength and will, saved Patrick McMahon's life.

Kennedy used his amazing imagination. With his knife, he cut off one end of a strap of leather, which was connected to McMahon's life jacket. Kennedy then bit down on the strap's end, and towed McMahon 3½ miles (5.8 km) to Plum Pudding Island.

MAP OF SOLOMON ISLANDS

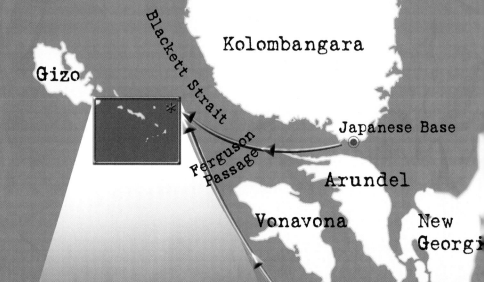

Kolombangara

Blackett Strait

Gizo

Japanese Base

Ferguson Passage

Arundel

Vonavona

New Georgi

U.S. Base

Rendo

CLOSE-UP OF CRASH SITE

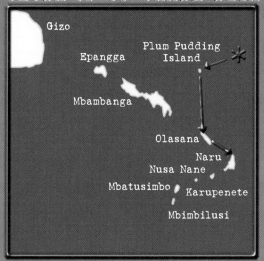

Gizo

Epangga

Plum Pudding Island

Mbambanga

Olasana

Naru

Nusa Nane

Mbatusimbo

Karupenete

Mbimbilusi

N

path of *Amagri*

path of PT109

JFK's swimming path

crash site

Three

Survivor's Island

It took the crew 4 hours to swim the 3½ miles to Plum Pudding Island. They hid among a group of trees near the shore. Moments later, a Japanese barge went by. Had the men not been hiding, they would have been spotted and taken as prisoners of war.

Night, August 2

Kennedy knew they couldn't wait on the island expecting that the navy would find them. He had to take action. That night, Kennedy swam into Ferguson Passage, hoping to find a patrolling PT boat. He wore only shoes, shorts, and a life jacket. For protection he had a .38 revolver. It hung around his neck from a string. He spent hours in Ferguson Passage. However, no PT boats appeared. Finally, he headed back for Plum Pudding Island.

These maps chart the course of events before and after PT109's collision with the *Amagri*.

Early Morning, August 3

On his swim back, Kennedy got caught in a current that swept him sideways into Blackett Strait. He started to make his way back to Plum Pudding Island once again. However, because he'd spent the night in the water, he was too weary to finish the swim. He stopped on a small island he'd seen on his swim out to Ferguson Passage. Overcome with fatigue, he just barely made it there.

Meanwhile, back on Plum Pudding Island, Kennedy's crew feared that the worst had happened to their young skipper.

Midday, August 3

When he woke, Kennedy was still weak. But he knew he had to get back to his crew. Kennedy pushed himself to his physical limits and willed himself back to Plum Pudding Island. He knew he couldn't make the trip again, so he asked Ross to try.

Night, August 3

Ross went out into Ferguson Passage. He left in the afternoon so that he wouldn't get lost in the dark. Ross's luck was no better than Kennedy's. He, too, saw no PT boats. After many hours in the water, Ross was tired. He swam to the small island where Kennedy had slept the night before.

Morning, August 4

In the morning, Ross returned to Plum Pudding Island. Even though Kennedy and the injured men were recovering, the crew was upset that help still hadn't come. Kennedy knew he had to do something to keep them from losing hope. If the men lost hope, he thought, they would lose their will to survive. If that happened, then surely they would die.

The crew survived on coconuts. They drank the milk and ate the meat. Their coconut supply, however, was quickly running out.

Early Evening, August 4

Kennedy decided that it would be better to move to another island. He led the men to Olasana Island. It was less than 2 miles (3.2 km) away. He had picked it for two reasons: Olasana Island was closer to Ferguson Passage and it had a fresh supply of coconuts. The night was cold and rainy. No one tried to go into Ferguson Passage. The exhausted men stayed huddled in the dark on Olasana.

Morning, August 5

The men were becoming more hopeless and angry. It appeared that the navy assumed that they had died when PT109 was sunk. Kennedy understood that if they were to be saved, they would have to do it themselves. He spoke with Ross, and they decided to swim to Naru Island. Naru Island was only a half mile away from Olasana Island. Kennedy hoped that his taking action would boost his crew's morale.

When Kennedy and Ross spotted an empty canoe on Naru Island, they worried that Japanese soldiers might be nearby.

When he and Ross reached the island, they found the wreckage of a Japanese vessel. Near the wreckage they found a box with Japanese writing on it. They were thrilled to find packets of crackers and candy inside. Kennedy knew this would raise his crew's spirits.

They continued exploring the island. Soon, they came upon a canoe. At the same time, two local people landed on Naru Island about a mile from Kennedy and Ross. Biuku and Eroni were natives who worked for the local coastwatcher. The job of coastwatchers was to spy on the Japanese and report what they saw to the U.S. Navy.

From across the beach, the two sets of men spotted each other. They each thought the other was Japanese. Kennedy and Ross dived for cover. Biuku and Eroni fled in their canoe. Kennedy and Ross stayed hidden to see if the enemy would show. When none did, they continued exploring Naru Island.

Night, August 5

Hoping to find a PT boat, Kennedy and Ross used the canoe they'd found on Naru Island to return to Ferguson Passage. They saw nothing, and their spirits sank. On their way back, they were caught in a brutal rainstorm. Their canoe capsized, or flipped over. They had to swim back to Naru Island. It was tough going, but Kennedy refused to let his men down. He had to find a way of being rescued. Down but not defeated, Kennedy and Ross spent the night on Naru Island.

Biuku and Eroni played a major role in the rescue of the PT109 crew. ▶

Four

Rescued!

Morning, August 6

Kennedy and Ross returned to the others on Olasana. Kennedy was surprised to see two natives with the crew. He would learn later that these were the same two he and Ross had encountered the previous day on Naru. In a stroke of great luck, Biuku and Eroni had stopped on Olasana and stumbled upon the other nine survivors. Thom had convinced Biuku and Eroni that he and the others wouldn't harm them.

Using hand gestures and a few words, Kennedy convinced Biuku and Eroni to take messages back to the PT base on Rendova. Kennedy wrote his message on a coconut shell.

Afternoon, August 7

On their way to the PT base, Biuku and Eroni let the coastwatcher they worked for know about

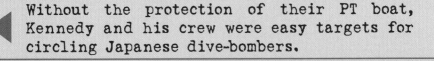

Without the protection of their PT boat, Kennedy and his crew were easy targets for circling Japanese dive-bombers.

Did you know?

When Kennedy was president, the coconut shell had a place of honor on his White House desk.

Kennedy and his crew. The coastwatcher sent seven native scouts to find the men. The scouts brought food and water to the starved men. The scouts also had a message for Kennedy. He was to go with them to meet the coastwatcher. Kennedy agreed, even though he knew he'd be in grave danger. Japanese planes would be flying right above him. Kennedy sprang into action.

To avoid being seen, he had to hide in the bottom of the canoe, covered with leaves. The planes circled the area around the canoe again

Kennedy sent a call for help on this simple coconut shell.

and again. Kennedy didn't dare move a muscle. With the slightest movement, the pilots would spot him and shoot to kill. Finally, the planes flew away. Kennedy had survived another dangerous situation.

Night, August 7

Kennedy reached the coastwatcher around 6:00 P.M. He arranged with the coastwatcher and naval officials to meet up with a PT boat in Ferguson Passage. He met up with PT157 sometime after 10:00 P.M. Kennedy directed PT157 to retrieve his crew on Olasana.

Kennedy's brave actions and steady leadership earned him the Navy and Marine Corps medal and the Purple Heart.

Morning, August 8

PT157 reached the survivors after midnight. The men cheered. PT157 returned to Rendova Harbor as the sun rose. John F. Kennedy had done the impossible—he had saved his crew.

THE AFTERMATH

The injured men received medical attention. Kennedy was given the chance to go home, but turned it down. He felt he still had much to accomplish in the South Pacific. He was given command of another boat, PT59. His heroism, however, came at a cost. Because Kennedy immediately accepted another command, there was not enough time for his injured back to heal. Kennedy's back suffered further damage. Pain would bother him for the rest of his life.

The other PT109 crew members were reassigned to other ships. Due to their injuries, McMahon and Johnston were unable to continue serving in the navy. They were sent home.

John F. Kennedy and the crew of PT109 had faced death head-on and won. None of them would ever forget the seven days they endured as survivors of a sunken ship.

NEW WORDS

ambassador an official representative of a
country

barge a flat boat that carries supplies

bow the front part of a ship or boat

capsized when a boat is flipped over

coastwatchers people who spied on the
Japanese and reported what they saw to
the U.S. Navy

current a forceful flow of water

destroyer a small battleship

dive-bombers Japanese fighter planes

general quarters the command given for a
ship's crew to get ready for battle

heroism showing courage and bravery

NEW WORDS

hull the body of a boat

malaria an illness spread by mosquitoes

morale a feeling of confidence and hope

propeller the blades of a torpedo that move
it forward

PT boat a small, fast, wooden boat armed
with torpedoes

starboard the right side of a ship

torpedo a self-propelled underwater weapon
used to sink ships

wake the path left in the water by a moving
ship or boat

warhead the part of a torpedo with
the explosives

RESOURCES

Web Sites
John F. Kennedy's Naval Service
http://www.history.navy.mil/faqs/faq60-2.htm
This site is part of the U.S. Navy's Web site. It features the navy's report on the sinking of PT109 as well as John F. Kennedy's naval records.

PT Boats, Inc.
http://www.ptboats.org
Find PT boat facts, photos, links, and news on this site. It is run by PT Boats, Inc., an organization established by PT boat veterans of World War II.

Knights of the Sea: PT Boats of World War II
http://www.geocities.com/Pentagon/4017/
This site has stories, action reports, photos, a list of medal winners, and links to other PT boat Web sites.

RESOURCES

Organizations
John F. Kennedy Library and Museum
Columbia Point
Boston, MA 02125

PT Boats, Inc.
P.O. Box 38070
Memphis, TN 38183

FOR FURTHER READING

Donovan, Robert J. *PT 109: John F. Kennedy in WWII*. New York: McGraw-Hill Professional Publishing, 2001.

Green, Michael. *PT Boats*. Manakato, MN: Capstone Press, 1999.

Spies, Karen Bornemann. *John F. Kennedy*. Berkeley Heights, NJ: Enslow Publishers, Inc., 1999.

When the *Amagri* struck PT109, the crew members were stationed throughout the boat. Upon impact, they were scattered into the dark, open seas. The names and ranks of the crew members are listed below, along with their location when PT109 was rammed.

Captain, John F. Kennedy
At the wheel, in the cockpit
Radioman, second class, John E. Maguire
Monitoring the radio in the cockpit
Quartermaster, third class, Edgar E. Mauer
Behind the cockpit, scanning for other PT boats
Ensign, Leonard J. Thom
On the deck
Ensign, George H.R. Ross
Manning the 37-millimeter gun at the front of the deck
Seaman, first class, Raymond Albert
In the middle of the ship, on lookout duty

Motor Machinist's Mate, first class, Patrick McMahon
In the engine room
Motor Machinist's Mate, first class, Gerald Zinser
Near the engine room
Motor Machinist's Mate, second class,
William Johnston
Near the engine room
Gunner's Mate, third class, Charles A. Harris
On break, lying near a torpedo tube
Torpedoman's Mate, second class, Raymond Starkey
On lookout duty near the rear of the boat
Motor Machinist's Mate, second class,
Harold W. Marney
Manning the forward gun turret
(killed in collision)
Torpedoman's Mate, second class, Andrew J. Kirksey
In back of the boat on the starboard side
(killed in collision)

INDEX

INDEX

About the Author

Philip Abraham is a freelance writer. He lives in New York City.